The I Don't Want to Go to School Book

By Alan Gross
Illustrated by Mike Venezia

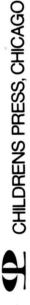 CHILDRENS PRESS, CHICAGO

Dedicated to the kids of Eisenhower Elementary School,
Crown Point, Indiana.

A.G. & M.V. '82

Library of Congress Cataloging in Publication Data

Gross, Alan, 1947-
The I don't want to go to school book

Summary: A youngster thinks that staying home
would be a perfect way to avoid the unpleasant things
that could happen during the school day. On the other
hand, what would he be missing?

[1. School stories] I. Venezia, Mike, ill.
II. Title.
PZ7.G899Id   [Fic]   81-17034
ISBN 0-516-03496-0   AACR2

Copyright© 1982 by Regensteiner Publishing Enterprises, Inc.
All rights reserved. Published simultaneously in Canada.
Printed in the United States of America.

7 8 9 10 R 91 90 89 88

I think I'd better not go to school today.

Yes, maybe I don't feel well.

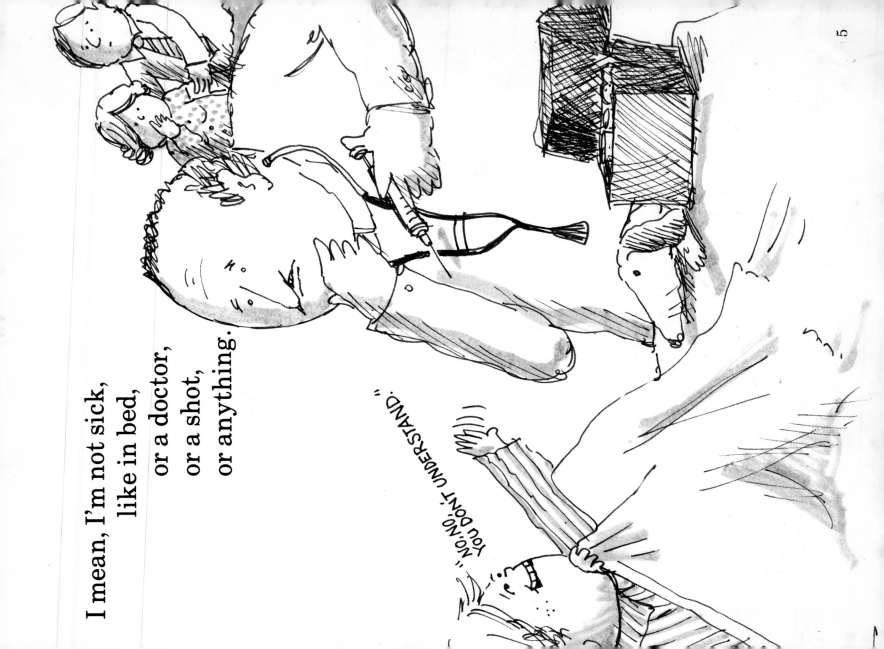

I mean, I'm not sick,
like in bed,
    or a doctor,
    or a shot,
    or anything.

"NO, NO, YOU DON'T UNDERSTAND."

Maybe, I'm just not well enough to spend another day in school.

What if I forget my bus money?

What if I get all sweated up in gym class?

"ATTA BOY," BRUCE!

Or have to wrestle with Big Bruce Novak again?

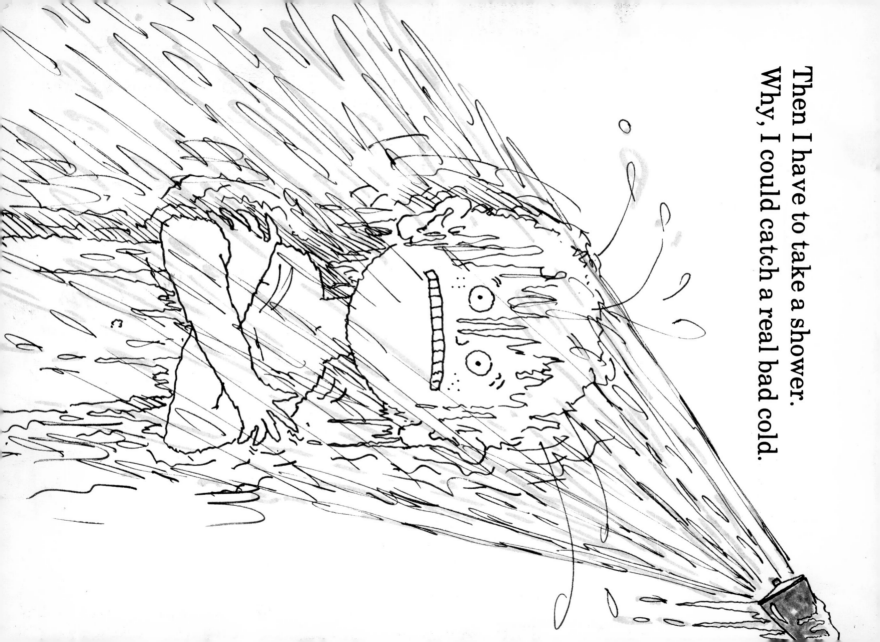

Then I have to take a shower.
Why, I could catch a real bad cold.

Or get snapped with a towel by the older kids.
Or just plain embarrassed to death.

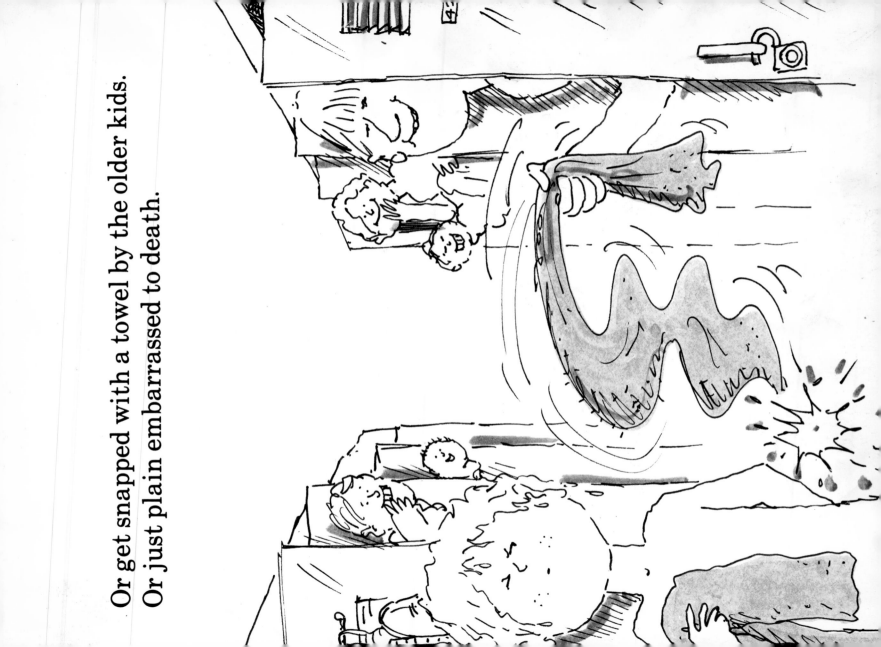

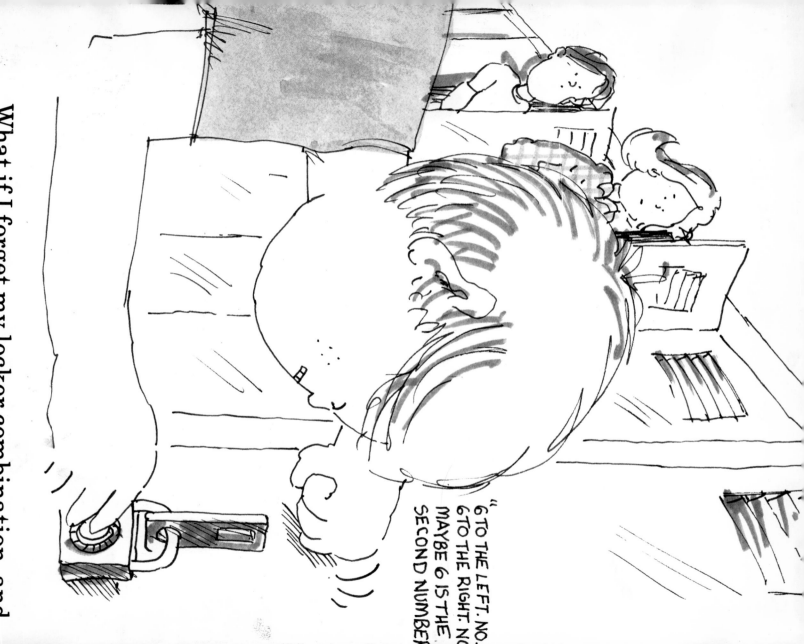

What if I forget my locker combination, and the teacher has to look it up, again?

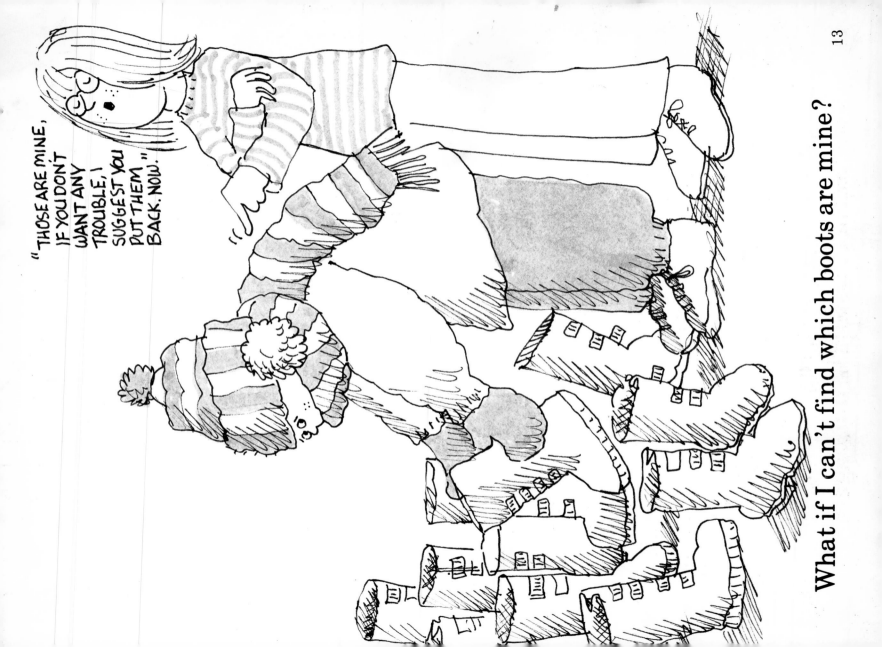

What if I can't find which boots are mine?

And after I find them, I can't get them on my feet, and my coat starts getting real hot.

"URRRRG!"

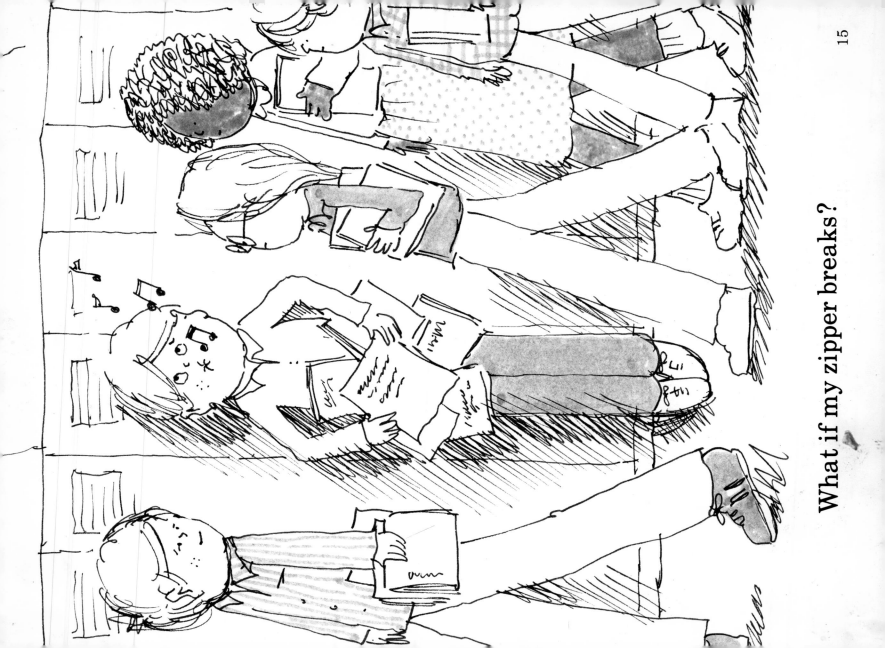

What if my zipper breaks?

And what if somebody throws up again? That could kill a day, right there.

What if I get reported by the crossing guards
for something I didn't even do?

What if I get caught passing a note and have to read it aloud to everybody?

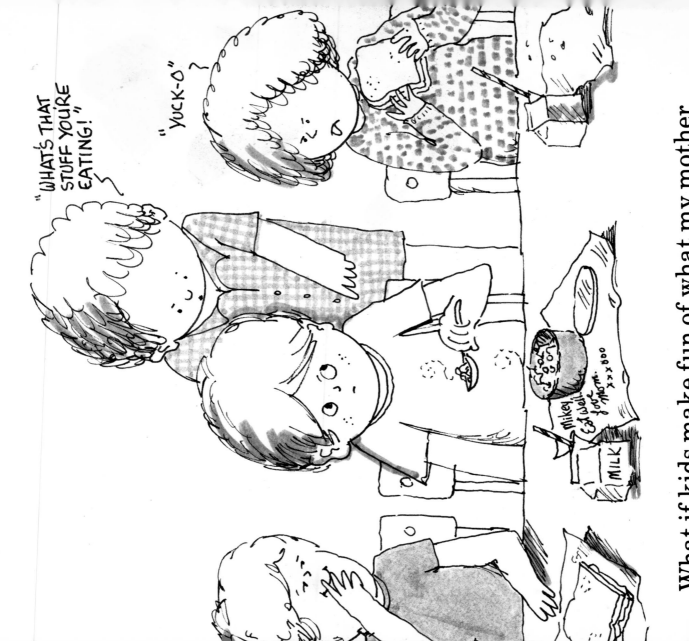

What if kids make fun of what my mother made for my lunch?

What if I have to go to the bathroom and I have to hold up my hand and everybody knows why?

So, maybe it's better if I just stay home today.

Of course, I won't get to see any of my friends, then.

If I stay in all day I can't go out after school.

And let's face it, there's nothing to watch on TV on a weekday.

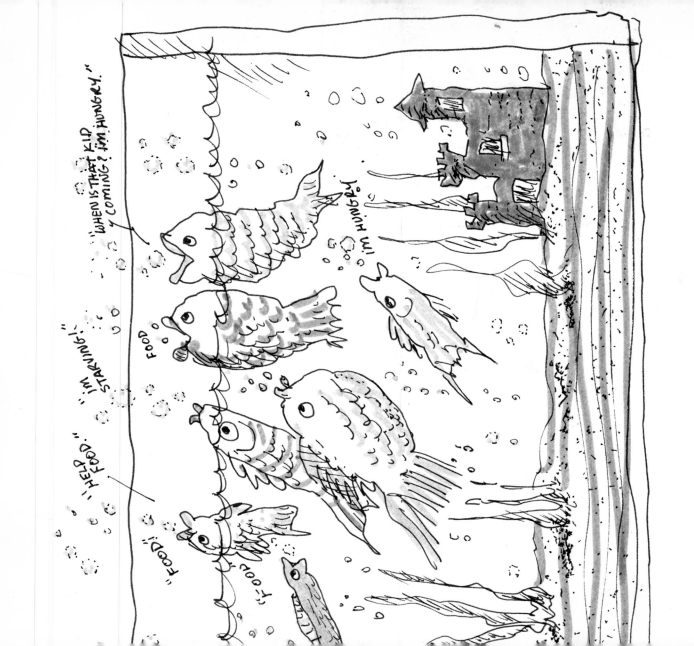

And who's going to feed the homeroom fish?
They're counting on me.

I mean, my desk is there with all my stuff in it.

And, sometimes the teacher is funny, and she shows us pictures of dinosaurs and stuff. . . . .

Sometimes we work with clay.

"THANK YOU, IT'S FOR MY MOM."

"THAT'S VERY CREATIVE."

28

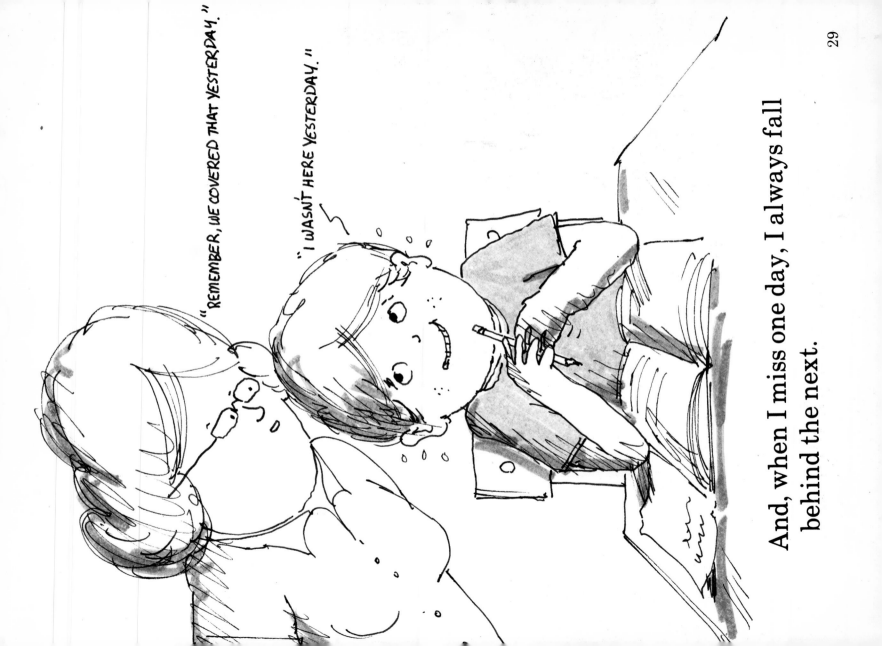

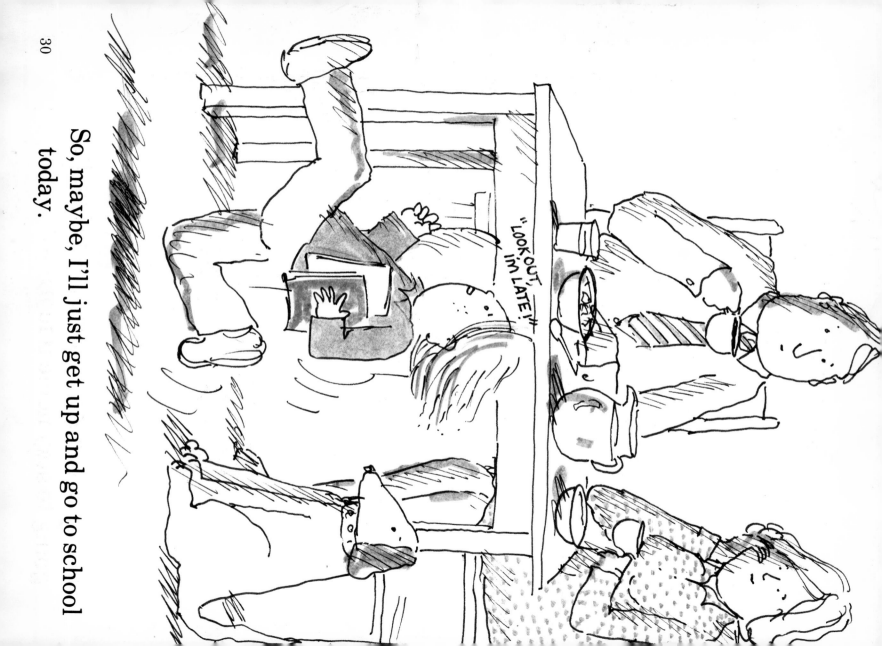

So, maybe, I'll just get up and go to school today.

But if school doesn't work out today, I'm going to stay home tomorrow.

MIKE

ALAN

ABOUT THE AUTHOR AND ARTIST:

The I Don't Want to Go to School Book is the third book by Alan Gross and Mike Venezia for Childrens Press. The others are *Sometimes I Worry* (1978) and *What If The Teacher Calls On Me?* (1980).

Alan Gross and Mike Venezia first met in 1970 while writing and designing television commercials for the Pillsbury Doughboy. They have also joined forces for Nestles Chocolate and many of the Kellogg's cereal brands. Both are native Chicagoans with solid backgrounds in children's advertising — good children's advertising, that is.

Alan, the writer, studied journalism and creative writing at the University of Missouri. He dropped out of graduate school to be an actor. Three of his plays have been produced in Chicago, *Lunching, The Phone Room,* and *The Man in Room 605.*

Alan is also a teacher and contributing editor to *Chicago Magazine.*

Mike, the illustrator, graduated from The School of the Art Institute in Chicago. His paintings have been shown in various galleries around Chicago.

When not working on kid's books, Mike is a busy Chicago Art Director and father of Michael Anthony and Elizabeth Ann.